Samuel de Champlain

Written by Elizabeth MacLeod

Illustrated by John Mantha

Kids Can Press

Imagine sailing across a huge ocean — and not knowing what you will find on the other side.

What would it be like to meet people with food and clothing that were very different from yours?

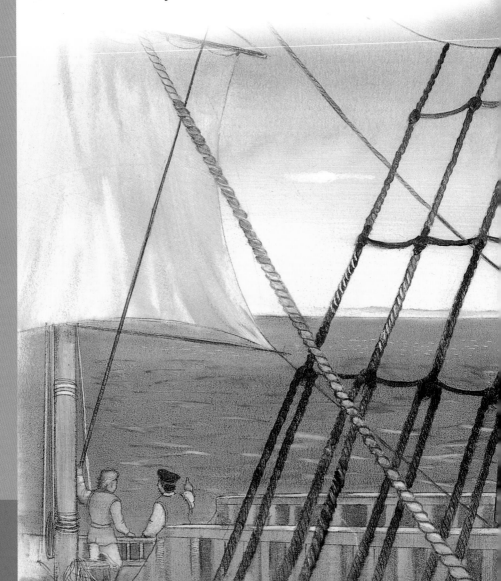

Explorers of long ago were brave people who visited faraway lands.

One of the most famous explorers lived more than 400 years ago. His name was Samuel de Champlain.

Samuel was born around 1580 in France. His father was a sailor. Samuel wanted to become a sailor, too.

When he grew up, Samuel became a soldier. A few years later, he did become a sailor, just as he had dreamed.

In 1599, Samuel sailed far from home. He crossed the huge Atlantic Ocean.

On his trip, Samuel visited beautiful islands. He saw trees and animals that were new to him. Samuel painted pictures of these things and wrote about them, too.

After about two years, Samuel sailed back home to France. He visited the king. King Henri wanted to hear about all the wonderful things Samuel had seen.

Samuel loved exploring. He hoped to sail across the ocean again. Next time, he wanted to explore a place called Canada.

For many years, sailors from France had brought animal furs and fish back from Canada. Some of these sailors had explored a part of Canada. They called this part New France.

On March 15, 1603, Samuel set sail for New France.

It took Samuel and the other sailors more than two months to sail across the Atlantic Ocean.

Samuel was excited to finally reach New France. He wanted to learn all about Canada.

The people who lived in Canada looked very different from Samuel and his friends. They spoke different languages, too.

Right away, Samuel liked these people. Today we call them First Nations people. That is because they were some of the first people to live in Canada.

Samuel wanted to explore a big river that sailors called the River of Canada. Today we call it the Saint Lawrence River.

Samuel drew pictures and maps of the things he saw. He wrote about them, too.

Samuel returned to France. But he sailed back to Canada with more men the next year. This time, Samuel explored the land beside the Atlantic Ocean.

While Samuel explored, the men built a fur-trading post. It was in the part of Canada that today we call New Brunswick.

The First Nations people had furs from beaver, fox and other animals. Samuel and the other men from France wanted the furs so they could sell them back in France.

The First Nations people did not have metal tools or wool blankets. At the fur-trading post, they could trade their furs for tools and blankets from France.

After exploring for about a month, Samuel returned to the fur-trading post. The group got ready to spend its first winter in Canada.

The winter was freezing cold. There
was little food.

When spring finally came, Samuel was
still alive. But 35 of the 79 men with him
—almost half—had died.

During the summer of 1605, Samuel explored along the ocean again. He was looking for a better place to live.

Samuel returned to his men in September. They moved to a place nearby called Port-Royal. The new place was less windy. It would not be so cold when winter came.

The First Nations people helped the men from France. They told Samuel and the others what plants and animals were good to eat.

The First Nations people also shared their food. That winter, only a few of Samuel's friends died.

The next fall, Samuel and some of his men again went exploring along the ocean.

When Samuel returned to Port-Royal, he started a club called the Order of Good Cheer. Every day, one of the men created a feast. Each man tried to make the best meal. The men were busy, happy and full.

King Henri wanted Samuel to build another fur-trading post in Canada. So in 1608, Samuel and some other men explored the Saint Lawrence River a second time.

On July 3, Samuel chose a place beside the river to build the new trading post. This place was in a part of Canada that the First Nations people called Quebec.

The First Nations people who lived there had invented many useful things. Their canoes and snowshoes made getting around much easier.

Samuel and his men learned how to use these inventions. First Nations people known as the Hurons taught them how. (Hurons were also called the Wendat.)

Samuel became good friends with many First Nations people. Some asked Samuel for help fighting their enemy, a First Nations group called the Iroquois (EAR-oh-kwa). Samuel agreed to help.

When Samuel and his First Nations friends met the Iroquois, the men from France raised their guns. Samuel killed two Iroquois chiefs.

The Iroquois had never seen guns before. They decided not to fight and ran into the woods.

Over the years, Samuel sailed back to France many times. Sometimes he returned with food, farm animals and tools. He also brought more people to live in New France.

Samuel kept exploring Canada. Huron guides helped him.

One day, the Hurons asked Samuel to paddle through some rough water with them. That showed they thought their friend was brave.

Samuel's Huron friends were happy when he made it. So was Samuel — he could not swim!

In 1615, Samuel and the Hurons were fighting the Iroquois. The battle took place in the land we now call New York State.

Samuel was hurt in the battle. A Huron soldier had to carry him to safety. Samuel spent the winter with the Hurons.

When Samuel arrived back in Quebec the next summer, his friends were amazed. They thought he had died.

Samuel was still helping Quebec to grow. In 1628, he got good news. Ships full of food, tools and more people were coming from France.

Soon Samuel heard that pirates from England had taken over the ships.

The English pirates stopped the ships because England and France were enemies.

Then some of the pirates went to see Samuel. They said that he and all the people from France had to leave Quebec. Samuel angrily said no.

Samuel and his friends had little food that winter. When summer came, the pirates again told everyone from France to leave. This time, Samuel sadly agreed.

The pirates took Samuel and the others back across the ocean. Would Samuel ever see Quebec again?

In 1632, the king of England finally agreed to let the king of France be in charge of New France.

So in the spring of 1633, Samuel returned to Quebec. Finally he was back in the land he loved.

Samuel spent the rest of his life in Quebec. He died there on December 25, 1635.

Samuel had worked to build trading posts. He had built towns and explored the land. Because of all his hard work, people today call Samuel "the Father of New France."

More facts about Samuel

- Samuel de Champlain was born around 1580. He died on December 25, 1635.

- Some of the First Nations groups Samuel met when he first arrived in Canada were the Hurons, the Mohawks and the Mi'kmaq (MIG-maw).

- Samuel named a lake after himself — Lake Champlain.

- When Samuel was exploring in 1613, he dropped one of his tools. It is now at the Canadian Museum of Civilization.

Visit www.kidscanpress.com for more information